Table of Contents

Shredded and Diced Veggies

    Wild Rice and Bacon Frittata

    Hide 'n' Seek Pizza

    Tortellini Bake

    Veggie Patch Patties

    Hash Brown Casserole

    Corn Fritters

Mashed and Pureed Veggies

    Cauliflower Crust Pizza

    Chock-Full Soup

    Cheesy Quiche

    Freeze-Friendly Chicken Nuggets

    Buttery Pudding

    Cheesy Sticks

    Garden and Ranch Dip

    Squish-Squash French Toast

    Oatmeal for Anyone

    Nutty 'Nana Coconut Waffles

    Harvest Pancakes

    Confetti Bread

    Best Homestyle Mac

    Party Poppers

    Island Paradise Smoothie

Dark Chocolate Cake

Ooey-Gooey Brownies

Wild Rice and Bacon Frittata

Sneaky Veggies: Onion

Ingredients

2 c. quick-cook wild rice

4.5 c. water

4 slices Prosciutto

7 eggs

1 c. finely sliced onion

2 c. finely sliced mushrooms

1 Tbsp. parsley

1 tsp. rosemary

1/4 tsp. black pepper

1/4 tsp. salt

4 slices prosciutto

1/3 c. shredded Parmesan

Directions

1. In a medium sauce pan, combine rice and water. Cook until tender and set aside.

2. While rice cooks, preheat oven to 350 degrees.

3. Whisk eggs, onions, mushrooms, and all spices until frothy and well combined. Pour egg mixture into pie pan.

4. Place prosciutto on a baking sheet lined with parchment paper. Bake for 11 – 13 minutes, or until crispy.

6. Bake egg mixture for 25 minutes, then sprinkle Parmesan on top and bake another 5 minutes.

7. After prosciutto is cool and before quiche is cooked through, roughly chop prosciutto. Sprinkle on top of quiche and serve immediately.

Hide and Seek Pizza

Sneaky Veggies: Tomatoes, Onions, Bell Peppers, Zucchini

Ingredients

2 lbs. tomatoes, roughly chopped

1/3 onion, roughly chopped

2 cloves garlic, minced

2 Tbsp. olive oil

1 Tbsp. basil

1 tsp. oregano

1/4 tsp. salt

1/4 tsp. black pepper

1 tsp. corn starch

1 ready-made pizza crust

2 red bell peppers, thinly sliced

1 medium zucchini, peeled and thinly sliced

2 c. shredded mozzarella

1 pack of pre-sliced pepperoni

Directions

1. In a medium sauce pan, combine tomatoes and onions. Cook on low about 3 hours.

2. Blend cooked tomatoes and onions until pureed. Add back to pan with garlic, oil, spices, and corn starch. Cook on low for 1 hour.

3. Preheat oven to 375 degrees.

4. Spread warm sauce on pizza crust. Arrange a layer of bell peppers, then a

layer of zucchini, on top of the sauce.

5. Cover with mozzarella, then top with pepperoni. Bake for 15 minutes or until cheese is bubbly.

Tortellini Bake

Sneaky Veggies: Broccoli, Tomatoes, Kale

Ingredients

2 Tbsp. olive oil

20 oz. pre-cooked cheese tortellini

1.5 c. spaghetti sauce

1 c. fresh broccoli, finely chopped

1 c. tomatoes, finely chopped

1 c. fresh kale, thinly shredded

2/3 c. mozzarella, shredded

1/2 c. Parmesan, finely shredded

1/2 c. breadcrumbs

Directions

1. Preheat oven to 375 degrees.

2. Grease an 8 x 12-inch casserole dish with half of the oil. Arrange a single layer of tortellini in the pan.

3. Pour a layer of spaghetti sauce on top of the tortellini.

4. Add broccoli, tomatoes, and kale in another layer. Dust with a small amount of parmesan cheese.

5. Arrange another layer of tortellini, then sauce, vegetables, and cheese.

6. Repeat layering until all tortellini, sauce, and vegetables are in the dish.

7. Cover entire top with mozzarella, then dust with breadcrumbs and drizzle with remaining olive oil.

8. Bake for 25 – 35 minutes, or until top is brown and cheese is bubbly. Serve hot.

Veggie Patch Patties

Sneaky Veggies: Onions, Zucchini

Ingredients

1 lb. lean ground beef

2 eggs

1/2 medium onion, minced

1 clove garlic, minced

1/2 zucchini, peeled and finely shredded

4 Tbsp. Worcestershire sauce

1/2 c. breadcrumbs

Salt and pepper to taste

Vegetable or canola oil for frying

Directions

1. In a large mixing bowl, whisk eggs, onions, garlic, salt, pepper, and Worcestershire sauce. Once those are mixed, add beef, zucchini, and breadcrumbs. Mix until well incorporated.

2. By hand or using a mold, form 6-oz. patties that are about 3/4" thick. Press a thumb indentation into the center.

3. In a large frying pan, warm oil on medium-high heat. Add patties in a single layer.

4. Cook patties on one side for about 2-1/2 minutes. Flip, and cook on the other side for the same amount of time.

5. Place on a warm bun and add your favorite toppings. Serve hot.

Hash Brown Casserole

Sneaky Veggies: Sweet potatoes, Squash, Potatoes

Ingredients

1 lb. sweet potatoes

1 lb. butternut squash

1 lb. gold potatoes

4 c. water

1-1/2 sticks butter, separated

1-1/2 c. low-fat milk

1 c. breadcrumbs

Salt and pepper to taste

Directions

1. Peel and wash potatoes and squash. Shred into hash brown strips with a mandolin (vegetable slicer).

2. Add strips to water and boil for 5 minutes or until they begin to soften. Drain.

3. Preheat oven to 375 degrees and melt 1 stick of butter in a small pan.

4. Stir melted butter and milk into potato and squash shreds. Season with salt and pepper.

5. Add potato and squash mix to a casserole dish. Toss remaining butter and breadcrumbs together, and top casserole with breadcrumb mix.

6. Bake uncovered for about 35 minutes or until browned on top. Allow to stand for 10 minutes before serving.

Corn Fritters

Sneaky Veggies: Zucchini, Onion

Ingredients

1 c. zucchini, peeled and shredded

1/4 c. onion, minced

1/2 c. frozen corn, thawed

1 egg

1-1/2 c. breadcrumbs

1 Tbsp. low-fat milk

Salt and pepper to taste

Vegetable or canola oil for frying

Directions

1. In a large mixing bowl, combine all ingredients until well incorporated.

2. By hand or with a mold, make patties of about 3 inches across and 3/4" thick.

3. In a skillet, warm oil over medium heat. Place patties at least 1" apart in the skillet and cook about 3 minutes on each side, or until well browned.

4. Serve hot with your choice of toppings, like sour cream, salsa, or butter.

Cauliflower Crust Pizza

Sneaky Veggies: Cauliflower

Ingredients

1 head of cauliflower

3 cloves garlic

1-1/3 c. mozzarella, shredded

1/2 c. Parmesan, shredded

2 eggs

1 tsp. dried oregano

Directions

1. Preheat oven to 400 degrees and line a baking sheet with parchment paper.

2. Chop cauliflower into large chunks, then place them with garlic into a food processor. Process until a cauliflower "rice" forms.

3. Spread cauliflower in a thin layer on baking sheet, then bake for about 15 minutes or until it's cooked and starts to brown. Cool.

4. When cauliflower is cooled, combine it in a large mixing bowl with mozzarella, Parmesan, eggs, and oregano. Mixture should form a dough.

5. Line a pizza-baking pan with parchment paper. Press dough in an even layer. Cauliflower works best as a thin crust.

6. Bake crust for 20 to 24 minutes, or until it starts to brown. If the crust still seems moist, bake for an additional 2 to 5 minutes.

7. Allow crust to cool, then top with your favorite pizza toppings. Bake as normal.

Chock-Full Soup

Sneaky Veggies: Onion, Celery, Kale, Okra

Ingredients

1 medium onion

3 stalks of celery

2 cloves garlic

4 large kale leaves

1 c. frozen okra

2 medium gold potatoes

2 medium carrots

2 medium tomatoes

1 c. green beans

1 c. frozen corn

2 c. chicken broth

2 c. vegetable broth

2 c. water

Salt and pepper to taste

Directions

1. Peel and roughly chop onion, celery, kale, potatoes, tomatoes, and carrots.

2. In food processor, combine onion, celery, garlic, kale, and okra. Blend until smoothly pureed.

3. Add potatoes and carrots to a large pot and cover with water. Boil for 30 minutes or until vegetables start to get tender.

4. Add broth and puree, and stir until well combined. Add the rest of the vegetables.

5. Reduce heat to low and cook uncovered for at least one hour or until all vegetables are cooked through.

6. Serve hot with crackers, toast, or grilled cheese sandwiches.

Cheesy Quiche

Sneaky Veggies: Onion, Bell Pepper, Mushrooms, Zucchini, Tomato

Ingredients

1 pre-cooked pie crust

1 Tbsp. olive oil

1/2 medium onion, finely sliced

1/2 green bell pepper, finely sliced

1/2 c. mushrooms, finely sliced

1 zucchini, peeled and finely sliced

1 medium tomato, finely chopped

3 eggs

1/4 c. heavy cream

1-1/2 c. shredded cheddar cheese, separated

Salt and pepper to taste

Directions

1. Preheat oven to 375 degrees.

2. Heat a large skillet over medium-high heat. Add oil and allow to warm. Add onion, bell pepper, mushrooms, zucchini, and tomato, stirring frequently, for about 6 minutes. Remove from heat.

3. In a mixing bowl, whisk together eggs, heavy cream, salt, and pepper until frothy.

4. Spread 3/4 c. cheese on bottom of crust. Add cooked veggies, then egg mixture. Bake for about 20 minutes, or until eggs start to set.

5. Take quiche out of oven, top with remaining cheese, then put back into oven for another 20 – 25 minutes or until a toothpick inserted in the center comes out clean.

6. Allow to cool for 2 – 4 minutes before serving.

Freeze-Friendly Chicken Nuggets

Sneaky Veggies: Carrots, Zucchini, Onion

Ingredients

1 lb. boneless, skinless chicken breasts

1 medium carrot, chopped

1 medium zucchini, peeled and chopped

1/2 medium onion, chopped

2 cloves garlic, minced

1 Tbsp. celery salt

2 tsp. mustard powder

1/4 tsp. black pepper

1 c. white flour

1 egg

1 Tbsp. milk

1-1/2 c. panko breadcrumbs

Directions

1. In a food processor, pulse chicken breasts until roughly ground. Add carrot, zucchini, onion, garlic, salt, mustard powder, and black pepper until well combined.

2. Set up stations: one dish of flour, one dish of whisked egg and milk, and one dish of breadcrumbs.

3. Preheat oven to 400 degrees.

4. Spread out patty-sized amounts of the chicken mixture, and use cookie cutters to make fun-shaped nuggets. Press nuggets into flour, then dredge in egg mixture, and cover with breadcrumbs.

5. Do this until all the chicken mixture is formed into nuggets and placed on a

baking sheet.

6. Spray nuggets with cooking oil and bake for 10 – 15 minutes or until golden brown, turning halfway through.

7. Serve immediately or cool and freeze for up to two months.

Buttery Pudding

Sneaky Veggies: Avocados

Ingredients

4 avocados

1 c. plain, low-fat Greek yogurt

2 c. almond milk

4 Tbsp. sugar or sugar substitute

1 Tbsp. cardamom

Directions

1. Pit and peel avocados, then roughly chop.

2. Add avocado, yogurt, milk, sugar, and cardamom to a blender. Process until smooth and creamy.

3. Refrigerate and serve chilled.

Cheesy Sticks

Sneaky Veggies: Broccoli, Green Onions

Ingredients

2 c. fresh broccoli, chopped

1/4 c. green onions, chopped

2 c. water

1 c. breadcrumbs

1-1/2 c. shredded Colby Jack cheese

3 eggs

Directions

1. Steam broccoli in a double boiler over water until tender. Set aside to drain and cool.

2. Preheat oven to 375 degrees and line a baking sheet with parchment paper.

3. In a food processor, combine broccoli, green onions, breadcrumbs, cheese, and eggs. Pulse until well combined.

4. Press mixture out onto lined baking sheet in an even layer. Cut into sticks of about 1-1/2" x 4".

5. Bake for 25 minutes, flip, and bake for another 20 minutes, or until sticks are crispy and browned on the outside.

6. Serve warm or let cool and freeze for up to two weeks.

Garden and Ranch Dip

Sneaky Veggies: Cucumber, Celery

Ingredients

1 small seedless cucumber

1 stalk celery

2 c. plain low-fat Greek yogurt or sour cream

8 Tbsp. parsley flakes

4 tsp. dill flakes

3 tsp. garlic powder

3 tsp. onion powder

2 tsp. basil flakes

Directions

1. Peel and finely chop cucumber and celery.

2. Combine vegetables with yogurt or sour cream. Mix in spices.

3. Refrigerate and serve chilled. Pair with pretzels, baby carrots, or baked French fries.

Squish-Squash French Toast

Sneaky Veggies: Squash

Ingredients

1 c. butternut squash, cooked and pureed

1/3 c. almond milk

3 eggs

1 tsp. vanilla extract

1 Tbsp. honey

1 Tbsp. cinnamon

1 lb. thick, crusty bread, sliced (Challah, Brioche, and other egg breads work well)

Butter for the pan

Directions

1. In a large mixing bowl, whisk together squash, milk, eggs, vanilla, honey, and cinnamon.

2. Dredge bread in mixture, then leave to soak overnight.

3. Remove bread from bowl and pile on a plate. Allow bread to return to room temperature.

4. Heat griddle pan or large skillet on medium heat. Butter pan.

5. Place bread in a single layer on griddle. Cook until browned, then flip and cook until second side is browned.

6. Serve hot with more honey, powdered sugar, maple syrup, or fruit compote.

Oatmeal for Anyone

Sneaky Veggies: Sweet Potato; Squash and Apples; or Carrots

Ingredients

Oatmeal Base

1-1/2 c. rolled oats

1/3 c. brown sugar

1 large egg

2 c. milk

3 Tbsp. butter, separated

Variation 1

1 large sweet potato

1/3 tsp. cinnamon

1/3 tsp. nutmeg

1/3 tsp. cloves

Variation 2

1 c. butternut squash, diced

1 c. sweet apples, sliced

1 tsp. cinnamon

1/2 c. walnuts, chopped

Variation 3

2 c. carrots, diced

1/2 c. golden raisins

3 Tbsp. maple syrup

Directions

1. Preheat oven to 350 degrees and grease a casserole dish with 1 Tbsp. butter.

2. Precook vegetables, fruits, and spices in a sauce pan with 2 Tbsp. butter until fork tender.

3. Spread vegetable mixture on the bottom of casserole dish. Mix oats in with vegetable mix (adding nuts if applicable). Melt remaining butter in medium mixing bowl.

4. Combine melted butter, brown sugar, egg, and milk and whisk until well combined. Pour mixture over vegetables and oats, mixing until all ingredients are well combined.

5. Bake uncovered about 30 minutes, or until oatmeal is set.

6. Serve hot with cold milk.

Nutty 'Nana Coconut Waffles

Sneaky Veggies: Carrot

Ingredients

1 medium carrot

2 Tbsp. butter

6 Tbsp. coconut flour

1/4 tsp. baking soda

1/4 tsp. salt

4 eggs

1/2 c. coconut milk

2 Tbsp. room temperature coconut oil

1 tsp. vanilla extract

1 large spotted banana, mashed

Cooking spray

1 c. mixed nuts, chopped

Directions

1. Wash carrot and dice into very small pieces. In a small sauce pan, combine carrot and butter over medium heat. Cook until soft, then puree in food processor. Set aside to cool.

2. In a small bowl, combine flour, baking soda, and salt.

3. In a large mixing bowl, combine carrot puree, eggs, milk, coconut oil, vanilla, and banana. Mix together until well incorporated.

4. Add dry mix to wet and stir until a thick batter forms. Allow to sit while waffle maker heats.

5. Spray waffle maker with nonstick spray, then pour batter in and top with a small amount of nuts. Cook until golden brown.

6. Serve hot.

Harvest Pancakes

Sneaky Veggies: Pumpkin

Ingredients

3 c. flour

1/2 c. sugar or sugar substitute

1 c. dry milk powder

1/3 c. cornstarch

1 Tbsp. baking powder

1 tsp. baking soda

1 tsp. salt

2 eggs

2-1/2 c. low-fat milk

3/4 c. pureed pumpkin

1 tsp. ground allspice

2 tsp. ground cinnamon

Cooking spray for griddle

Directions

1. Combine all ingredients in a large mixing bowl and stir until a smooth batter forms.

2. Heat griddle to medium-high heat. Spray with cooking spray.

3. For each pancake, pour about 1/3 c. batter. Cook until bubbles start to form around the edges, about 3 minutes. Flip pancakes and cook another 3 minutes or until golden brown.

4. Serve hot with honey, maple syrup, or whipped cream.

Confetti Bread

Sneaky Veggies: Zucchini, Red Peppers, Green Onions

Ingredients

3 Tbsp. water

1-1/2 tsp. active dry yeast

2-2/3 c. bread flour, separated

1/2 c. buttermilk

2 Tbsp. canola oil

2 Tbsp. sugar or sugar substitute

1 tsp. salt

1/2 c. old fashioned oats

2/3 c. zucchini, shredded

1/4 c. red pepper, shredded

1 Tbsp. green onions, finely chopped

2 Tbsp. Romano cheese, grated

Directions

1. Warm water to about 75 degrees. In a large mixing bowl, dissolve yeast in warm water. Add in 2-1/2 c. flour, 1 Tbsp. oil, sugar, salt, oats, zucchini, red pepper, onions, and cheese to form a dough.

2. Grease a bowl with 1 Tbsp. oil. Flour a clean surface and dump dough onto it. Knead until elastic, about 9 minutes, then put into greased bowl. Turn once to grease both sides, then cover and leave to rise in a warm place about 1-1/2 hours, or until doubled.

3. Flour a clean surface, turn greased dough onto it, and divide dough in half. Shape each loaf into two greased loaf pans. Cover again and allow to rise until doubled again.

4. Preheat oven to 375 degrees. Bake loaves for 30 – 40 minutes, or until

golden brown on top. Cooked bread should sound hollow when tapped.

5. Cool on wire racks and serve with a meal or use for sandwich bread.

Best Homestyle Mac

Sneaky Veggies: Cauliflower, Carrots

Ingredients

4 c. dried macaroni

4 qt. water

2 Tbsp. olive oil

2 c. cauliflower, roughly chopped

2 medium carrots, roughly chopped

1 small onion, roughly chopped

1 egg

5 Tbsp. butter, separated

1/4 c. white flour

2-1/2 c. milk

1 lb. sharp cheddar cheese, shredded

Directions

1. Preheat oven to 350 degrees.

2. Bring water to boil, add macaroni, and allow to cook until al dente, about 8 minutes, stirring frequently. Remove from heat, drain (keeping the water), and toss in a bowl with olive oil.

3. Bring the pasta water back to a boil and cook cauliflower, carrots, and onions until tender. Remove from pot and place in a food processor. Pulse several times until nearly pureed.

4. In a small bowl, whisk the egg until frothy.

5. Add flour to a medium sauce pan with 4 Tbsp. butter, and cook over medium-low heat, whisking constantly, for 2 – 3 minutes. Slowly add the milk in, still whisking, until fully combined. Cook for 5 minutes or until it

becomes thick. Reduce heat to low.

6. Remove about 1/4 c. of the mixture and slowly pour it into the egg bowl, whisking constantly to avoid cooking the eggs, until smooth. Pour this into the sauce pot, still whisking, until well combined. Add the cheese and continue to whisk until it is fully melted.

7. Add the vegetable puree, still whisking constantly, until well combined. Add in macaroni and stir until totally coated with the sauce.

8. Grease a casserole dish with remaining butter. Pour in macaroni and cheese mix. Bake until bubbly and golden. Serve hot.

Party Poppers

Sneaky Veggies: Green Onions, Celery, Carrot, Leek

Ingredients

2 Tbsp. extra virgin olive oil

1/4 c. green onions, diced

1/2 celery stalk, diced

1 large carrot, diced

1/2 small leek, diced

3 fresh mushrooms, diced

1 garlic clove, minced

1 Tbsp. soy sauce

2 tsp. light brown sugar

1/3 c. sharp cheddar, shredded

2 eggs

1 c. breadcrumbs, separated

1/3 c. flour, seasoned with salt and pepper

Vegetable or canola oil for frying

Directions

1. In a large skillet, heat olive oil over medium-high heat. Sautee green onions, celery, carrot, leek, and mushrooms until soft, about 8 – 9 minutes. Add garlic and cook for an additional 1 – 2 minutes, until aromatic.

2. In a small bowl, combine soy sauce and brown sugar until well mixed. Pour mixture over cooked vegetables and stir until well coated. Remove from heat and allow to cool.

3. Pulse vegetables in a food processor until finely chopped. Transfer vegetable mix to mixing bowl and add cheddar, 2/3 c. bread crumbs, and 1

egg. Mix until well combined.

4. By the spoonful, form mixture into balls. (You can also make patties from which to cut shapes with cookie cutters.) Lay balls or shapes on a platter and cool for one hour in the refrigerator.

5. In a large skillet, heat enough vegetable or canola oil for frying over medium heat.

6. Set up three stations: one for flour, one for the remaining egg (whisked), and one for the remaining breadcrumbs.

7. Take the cooled balls or shapes from the refrigerator. Coat sides of ball with flour, dip in egg, then roll in breadcrumbs.

8. Fry for 2 minutes on each side or until outside is golden brown and crispy. Allow to drain on a wire rack. Serve warm with dip or by themselves!

Island Paradise Smoothie

Sneaky Veggies: Kale, Spinach

Ingredients

1/2 large banana

1 c. sliced peaches

1/2 c. pineapple chunks

2 c. fresh kale, washed

1 c. fresh spinach, washed

4 Tbsp. vanilla protein powder

Directions

1. Freeze fruits overnight for best smoothie consistency.

2. Add all ingredients to blender or food processor.

3. Pulse until well combined and smooth.

4. Serve chilled on a hot day!

Dark Chocolate Cake

Sneaky Veggies: Beets

Ingredients

3 c. beetroots

2/3 c. dark chocolate

3 eggs

2 c. coconut or light brown sugar

1 c. butter, melted

1 tsp. vanilla extract

1-1/2 c. almond meal

1-1/2 tsp. baking powder

1/2 c. powdered cacao or cocoa

1/4 tsp. salt

Cooking spray

Directions

1. Preheat oven to 350 degrees.

2. Wash beetroots thoroughly, then add to a pot with cold water. Bring water to boil, and allow to cook until beetroots are soft, about half an hour. Once they are cooked, rinse under cold water to take off the skins. Mash well, leaving some small lumps for texture.

3. Melt dark chocolate in a bowl in the microwave on low for about 1 minute. Quickly stir melted chocolate to liquefy any pieces that are still solid.

4. In a large mixing bowl, whisk together eggs, sugar, butter, and vanilla. Once those are well combined, slowly add in beetroot mash and melted chocolate.

5. Sift almond meal, baking powder, cacao, and salt in and mix until

combined. Be sure not to over-mix!

6. Coat an 8-inch cake pan with cooking spray, then pour in batter. Bake for 45 minutes to an hour, or until a toothpick pushed into the middle comes out clean.

7. Allow to cool in the pan. Serve alone or with cream cheese icing.

Ooey-Gooey Brownies

Sneaky Veggies: Eggplant

Ingredients

2 small eggplants

Salt for purging

Water to boil

12 oz. dark chocolate, chopped

Cooking spray

3-1/2 c. powdered cacao or cocoa

1/4 c. almond flour

2/3 c. honey

3 eggs

2 tsp. baking powder

1/3 c. walnuts, chopped

Directions

1. Slice, peel, rinse, and dice eggplant into small cubes. Generously salt it, then leave it to drain in a colander for 1 – 2 hours. Rinse well, then pat dry with paper towels.

2. Steam eggplant in a double-boiler until very soft. (Undercooking eggplant will make it bitter. The longer it cooks, the milder the taste will be.) Set aside to cool in a large bowl.

3. In a microwave-safe bowl, melt chocolate on low, stirring frequently, until fully liquefied.

4. Preheat oven to 350 degrees. Line a baking pan with lightly sprayed parchment paper.

5. Mash cooled eggplant, then stir in chocolate until well combined.

6. In a second mixing bowl, combine cacao, flour, honey, eggs, and baking powder. Whisk mixture until smooth. Add eggplant mix and walnuts. Stir just until combined.

7. Pour batter into pan and bake for about 45 minutes, or until a toothpick inserted into the center comes out clean.

8. Allow to cool 8 – 10 minutes before serving with a tall glass of cold milk.

Made in the USA
Las Vegas, NV
21 December 2021